MW00810232

# Object Lesson

Jennifer Jean

LILY POETRY REVIEW BOOKS

Published by Lily Poetry Review Books
223 Winter Street
Whitman, MA 02382

https://lilypoetryreview.blog/

ISBN: 978-1-7347869-8-9
Library of Congress Control Number: 2020937320

Cover art: *Self Discipline II: Pandemic Art* by Julie Shematz

*A bird doesn't sing because it has an answer,*
*it sings because it has a song.*

*—Maya Angelou*

# Contents

# Object Lesson

# INTRODUCTION

The commercial sex trade includes but is not limited to: sex trafficking, stripping, escorting, porn, and sugar dating or, it's sometimes even referred to as "sex work." Any time one human with money and status pays another human who doesn't have that same status for sex, it's considered exploitation.

You may have heard that age old saying that "Prostitution is the world's oldest profession." The reality is that prostitution is the world's oldest oppression against women and children. There is nothing glamorizing or empowering about the commercial sex trade. Growing up, I watched the movie Pretty Woman starring the beautiful Julia Roberts, and that shaped my idea of what women were like when they "chose" to make money that way.

Being in the commercial sex trade for eight years myself, not once did Richard Gere show up in a Lamborghini and put a string of pearls around my neck. On the contrary, I was emotionally, mentally, and spiritually dead for those years, and for many years to come. Like most women who enter the trade, I was young, naive, vulnerable, and looking for love. I met a handsome young man at a nightclub. He quickly groomed me into becoming his "bottom bitch." That's the term traffickers use for the victim in the number one spot. I had to cook, clean, take care of the entire house, and most importantly recruit or train the other women he would lure. I would end up prostituted all over New England in illicit massage parlors, high-priced hotels in Boston, private homes, and even in a legal brothel in Nevada. I never once loved what I was doing. I hated every moment of it, but I held on to hope because my trafficker promised me safety and security in things like a family, a nice home, and a business. Sadly, this never came to fruition and I lost my soul in the process.

Out of "the life" for 13 years, clean and sober, I would never trade my life for someone else's. Recovery has been horrible, beautiful, and messy. But I have learned how to turn my shame into my superpower by sharing my story in a transparent and authentic way. My hope is that you will read these poems with an open mind so that you can try to understand what it takes to come out of a life like that—to get a glimpse at just how resilient and brave these survivors are. I also recommend reading other survivors' stories so that you can share what you have learned with friends and family.

—Jasmine Grace Marino, founder and director of Bags of
Hope Ministries, and author of The Diary of Jasmine Grace

I am so over this
ancient itch! How sweet the reach

when I've been a *retch*
if you called me a sound. *O!*
*Amazing grace!*

# #CarryThatWeight

*Columbia senior Emma Sulkowicz has been hauling her own dorm mattress around campus every day [because] the student she says raped her is still free to attend the school without formal consequences.* —Amanda Hess in *Slate*

My mom was broken by five
or six guys one dawn before I was born.
That's gotta be the weight of
a king. & she carries that. Carried that
right past the police station on Burbank around noon.

I consider carrying our queen-sized
around our apartment
like those "Students for Emma!" from around the globe.
But I'm just a weaker
upper body.

I take on my daughter's futon.
My mom got it for her at Ikea. It's a lightweight.
& the idea
is to lug it for about an hour. At home.
Write as I go. Some kind of science, some kind of art.
In order
to relate.

My daughter moves stuffed dogs & pigs off her quilt,
helps me slide the pony colored twin onto my spine.
She makes me a tortoise.
She takes pictures, *Smile. Smile.*

*Smile.* I don't
think I can bear it a minute. It's hers.
My daughter's, my mother's, all
the grand hers.

& I won't
where I teach. I teach
so I'd mulled hauling it to the University. But
taking on a big thing like that? Sweating, bending

under that?
You know what lives under a bed.
All the weight

of my frame thumps the ground in the kitchen
as I dump the thing,
hard. My daughter rolls on it, giggles.
My pen's gone, &

my mom was broken
by five or six guys one dawn before I was born.

## Object Lesson

I say, *Hold in your yell*
*& face*
*the window,*
then place her objects in a long row
on her mussed-up bed.
At my *GO!*
my daughter
turns & strikes.

She doesn't hit
the plastic Appaloosa
with neon pink saddle,
or the boy-sized bear
in stained red hoodie,
or the pellet-filled pillow,
or her ratty, lime blankie.

She hits the American
Girl Doll. *Why?*

*She's like a person*
*& I'm mad at a person.*
(Some kind of science here,
some kind of art.)

So I say, *Now you've a chance to think—*
*what would you hit?*

*The pillow!* she says.
*Because you told me to hit things*
*when I'm mad.*
*Not people.*

I did!

& it's a soft thing,
she smiles,
*It can't hurt me.*

*When I taught poetry at the safe house,*

a kitten was lifted by the scruff
by one of the safe women.

She stroked, & stroked, &
it whirred,
& we read "Bitch"
by Carolyn Kizer.

& later I thought about how
that stroking woman once stirred
from an occupational
blackout & found a poem
in her scrawl.

She'd pressed its soul into memory—
then burnt its remains
in a Chinese bowl.
The smoke whirled from thieves.

She spoke the whole
in class today, to me
& to the other
sex-trafficking survivors.

She looked up & to the left.
Her tongue out at the corner
like a schoolgirl, like
a lioness. & I
liked it.

*O!* call me out—who
is, after all
this time, *a disaster*
*not to be found.*

## Exchange

*I can't believe these people,*
says Flannery. (Let's call her
Flannery.)

*They're building these casinos*
*so close to homes. Pimps make you*
*work*
*those hotels forever.*

Everyone in Starbucks
can hear
our exchange

over the blender & bustle. So,
I turn off
the recorder. Stop interviewing.
But Flannery keeps

musing,
*People notice nothing. I got beat*
*in one suite & thought for sure—*
*someone knows*
*& hears me bloody*
*murder screaming.*

*But—no—*

I nod, *Yeah…*
*people.* & I see her

bruise up
when, really, she matches her flan Frappuccino—
all okay, all foamy
& tawny-schemed
in drifting layers. We sip,
stare off.

\*

11

She says,
*A reporter once paid me to talk
about "the life." I open the door
& he gets up—off the bed!
We got, like, 5 minutes.*

I nod & turn & see
this retiree,
in racing shorts & pulled up tube socks.
He's totally listening.
He hasn't unstiffened

in his fireside armchair
in forever.

                    *

*I wonder if I can find him,* she says,
*Pay him to write a story.
To get the word out. I remember
he called me "Sunny."*

I say, *The paper pays him.*
&, I think about the two of us
working the power

of words. How, soon, I'll be
poeming. How Flannery wrote
an imitation of Afaa Weaver's "The Appaloosa"
in our safe home poetry class.

I think about this other time
at Starbucks,

when the wife of a colleague
leaned between
Flannery & me—

said, *Aren't you Jennifer?*

She came between me &
my notes, actually.
The interview was over.

   *

I don't tell Flannery
any of this. I stop
her story—decide,

*Next time,*
*let's talk in my car.*

## Object

*Debbie Does the Drawer.*
See?  It's a joke.
For some people
it's in the alliterative *d-d-d,*

it's nostalgia for that ancient porn
*Debbie does Dallas.*  Some people
laugh & laugh. See—
police search the apartment

but don't find Debbie.
Because…
Debbie does the drawer!
She's crushed

into a trundle
under a bed. She can cry
out.  She does not cry out
(the officer may not be the officer).

*

What about the one where
Debbie does a dog crate
for 40 days?
*Are you hungry*, they ask.

This fucking thing
can't be hungry—
they know that. It's a joke.
So they stick it & stick it

& stick it full
of dog biscuits.
Laugh & laugh. But
all jokes aside, they know

it is serious business.
The breaking down
biz, the wising up biz.
Want a thing, buy a thing.

Be the one to sell.
& the object can't object.

\*

*Bend over,* says a man
the first time, *I want to see
what I'm working with…*
The object

sometimes doesn't know
what it is, what to do—
but it will learn.
Its tongue hits the roof

& an open-mouthed hum,
a sort of "nnnnnnn"
precedes an "OH!"
But: no no no no no

no no no no no no….

the object can't object.
What's it for? Fifty
men a day or more.
Getting "the girlfriend experience"

or getting in getting off
going home.

\*

*Most of them were married,
with kids,* said Debbie
with a cup of cocoa,
debriefing, *& every single one*

*of them, I asked them*
*why they were coming…*
*they didn't have an answer*
*for me.*

# Garden of Truth

*A john said to me, "I thought we killed all of you."*
—from an interviewee in the Garden of Truth study
of trafficked Native Women in Minnesota

Are you dead yet? Are you dead yet? Are you dead yet? Are you dead yet? Are you
dead yet? Are you dead yet? Are you dead yet? Are you dead yet? *Can you see me?* Are
you dead yet? Are you dead yet? Are you dead yet? Are you dead yet? Are you dead
yet? Are you dead yet? Are you dead yet? Are you dead yet? Are you dead yet? *Can
you see me?* Are you dead yet? Are you dead yet? Are you dead yet? Are you dead yet?
Are you dead yet? Are you dead yet? Are you dead yet? Are you dead yet? Are you
dead yet? *No.* Are you dead yet? Are you dead yet? *Where is Canal Park?* Are you dead
yet? Are you dead yet? Are you dead yet? Are you dead yet? Are you dead yet? Are
you dead yet? Are you dead yet? Are you dead yet? Are you dead yet? Are you dead
yet? *Can you see me?* Are you dead yet? Are you dead yet? Are you dead yet? Are you
dead yet? Are you dead yet? Are you dead yet? Are you dead yet? Are you dead yet?
Are you dead yet? *Is this Seaway Hotel?* Are you dead yet? Are you dead yet? Are you
dead yet? Are you dead yet? *Where is my home?* Are you dead yet? Are you dead yet?
Are you dead yet? Are you dead yet? Are you dead yet? Are you dead yet? Are you
dead yet? Are you dead yet? Are you dead yet? Are you dead yet? Are you dead yet?
Are you dead yet? *No. Where is Canal Park?* Are you dead yet? Are you dead yet? Are
you dead yet? Are you dead yet? *Can you see me?* Are you dead yet? Are you dead yet?
Are you dead yet? Are you dead yet? Are you dead yet? Are you dead yet? Are you
dead yet? Are you dead yet? Are you dead yet? *Where is my home?* Are you dead yet?
Are you dead yet? Are you dead yet? Are you dead yet? Are you dead yet? *Can you
see me?* Are you dead yet? Are you dead yet? *Where is Canal Park?* Are you dead yet?
Are you dead yet? Are you dead yet? Are you dead yet? Are you dead yet? Are you
dead yet? Are you dead yet? Are you dead yet? Are you dead yet? *No.* Are you dead
yet? Are you dead yet? Are you dead yet? Are you dead yet? *What year is this?* Are you
dead yet? Are you dead yet? Are you dead yet? *Where is my home?* Are you dead yet?
Are you dead yet? Are you dead yet? Are you dead yet? Are you dead yet? *Can you
see me?* Are you dead yet? Are you dead yet? Are you dead yet? Are you dead yet? Are
you dead yet? *Is this Lake Superior?* Are you dead yet? Are you dead yet? Are you dead
yet? Are you dead yet? Are you dead yet? Are you dead yet? *Is this Seaway Hotel?* Are
you dead yet? Are you dead yet? Are you dead yet? Are you dead yet? Are you dead
yet? Are you dead yet? Are you dead yet? *What year is this?* Are you dead yet? *Can you
see me?* Are you dead yet? Are you dead yet? Are you dead yet? Are you dead yet? Are
you dead yet? Are you dead yet? Are you dead yet? Are you dead yet? Are you dead
yet? *Can you see me?* Are you dead yet? Are you dead yet? *No.* Are you dead yet? Are

you dead yet? Are you dead yet? *Where is my home?* Are you dead yet? Are you dead yet? Are you dead yet? Are you dead yet? Are you dead yet? Are you dead yet? Are you dead yet? Are you dead yet? Are you dead yet? Are you dead yet? Are you dead yet? *Is this Lake Superior?* Are you dead yet? Are you dead yet? Are you dead yet? *Can you see me?* Are you dead yet? Are you dead yet? Are you dead yet? Are you dead yet? Are you dead yet? Are you dead yet? Are you dead yet? *No.* Are you dead yet? Are you dead yet? *Where is my home?* Are you dead yet? *No.* Are you dead yet? Are you dead yet? Are you dead yet? *What year is this? Can you see me?* Are you dead yet? Are you dead yet? Are you dead yet? Are you dead yet? Are you dead yet? Are you dead yet? *Where is Canal Park?* Are you dead yet? Are you dead yet? Are you dead yet? Are you dead yet? *No. Where is Canal Park?* Are you dead yet? *No.* Are you dead yet? Are you dead yet? Are you dead yet? Are you dead yet? Are you dead yet? Are you dead yet? Are you dead yet? Are you dead yet? Are you dead yet? *No.* Are you dead yet? Are you dead yet? *Where is Canal Park?* Are you dead yet? Are you dead yet? Are you dead yet? Are you dead yet? Are you dead yet? Are you dead yet? Are you dead yet? Are you dead yet? Are you dead yet? Are you dead yet? Are you dead yet? Are you dead yet? Are you dead yet? *No.* Are you? *No.* Are you? *No.* Are you? *No.* Are you? *No.* Are you? *No.* Are you? *No.* Are you? *No.* Are you? *No.* Are you? *No.* Are you? *No.* Are you? *No. Can you see me?* No. *No.* No. *No*

Dear Jasz,

When you're just a little chick at the bar
& this regular dude from Roxbury jerks a jeweled hand out his pocket
to flash his thick wad—

don't think you can play him.
He knows you.

& later, when you're down your first day hooking,
down fourteen hours in a windowless "salon" in CT,
when you're in his jag to Cambridge,
holding a new, limp wad in your hand—

see how small it is.
Remember—this isn't your money.

Think about how money burns.

& when he parks & gets out, & you get out,
& you two meet near the trunk of the jag
in the dark of the morning—
he'll hold open his jeweled hand & ask, *Is this gonna be a problem?*
Tell him, *Hell yeah!* & walk away.

But when you beat your truth bloody,
when you pass the cash & tell him, *No…it won't.*
Try to mean, *No it won't, because*

*what I did for one, or a thousand days cannot ruin me.*
& mean it. Then walk away.

But don't go to Revere.
He knows where you live.

& when you don't walk away, don't break your rules
back in that hole in CT.
When you do break
those rules, like when
you let that bald dude choke you—

understand: there's no one home to lock up, you're not there anymore
to say NO
to this shit or that piss—

your soul is gone & safe & sleeping.
& you will surely die
if it's really YOU shutting the door to the moldy blue room no girl wants
in that "salon" in CT.

But when it's shut it's
shut it's shut it's shutting you in
with a father of a daughter. With some mother's son.

Let yourself think that—
think, *This guy has kids.*
Even as you swallow upchucked acid, swallow their wad.
This thought keeps them human—

& if they're human like you
then you might forgive them

someday.

& later when you're out of the life & your soul returns,
let it hurt to be home.
Don't use.

When you stop using
know it's a sign that you've never heard of the word "sober."

& later, when you've got your own place, & a kid, & job that needs a pantsuit,
& you're thinking about forgiveness
a little,

& you're in that Saugus church basement
with these women warriors & some weak coffee
—you're with Barb who brings Christmas baskets to strippers on Route One—

& you lift your mug for a sip & hear this clear lyric, this
*Swinnnng lowwwww, sweet chaaaarioooot...*

Don't ignore it.
Some long gone, former slaves are singing
about *the brightest day.*

"Escort" is her word &

the whole interview's about her girl.

D says, *I wanted her to know*
*but know my way,*

*not at school or from some jerk.*
*So one day I say, "We should talk," & she's freaked.*

*We sit down in the kitchen &*
*she starts crying. (So I'm thinking,* She knows…*)*

*"You got Cancer!*
*You got Cancer!" she starts screaming.*

D snorts, *We laugh about it now.*

*How she was so relieved*
*I wasn't*
*dying.*

*

Others in town talk
about D's son

finding her nude online, or
fellow yacht-clubbers finding her & showing him
her webcam antics, her customer ratings
on her "Escort" ads.

*My son was bound,*
says D,
*to notice*

*my overnight bag. I stuffed it*
*with lingerie.*
*I mean—*
*jeez…*

she shrugs.

There's a bit of dead
air for the boy, then
he's gone

from the interview.

＊

D scans the Starbucks
where we perch on stools. Says she's failed
the bar exam a lot, her ex is a nerd,
that she wants another degree
& to write a memoir,
*But I'm so exhausted!*

Then it's back to her girl, *When I take my girl*
*on errands, I point out*
*all the jerks in town who're clients &*
*we laugh. An orgasm*
*is like a pedicure for these guys.*
*I mean—jeez…*

*Who does that?*

she shakes out her long, frosted hair.
She's fifty-three, so she's got some grey,
but it looks classy.

I wonder if she'll start pointing.

＊

Instead, D looks back at me.
*One time we saw this big ass politico*
*I've known for years*
*slurping pancakes with his wife at IHOP.*

She says his name
& I'm ready to stop the recorder.
*Too funny,* she sighs. She's so

far away she squints
at me, says, *My girl's cool.* I nod.
*We talk about all our guys.*
*It's all good.*

*

*Just wish there wasn't*
*side effects.* She leans away
but we're closer now—like mother,
like daughter. & the monied men
in Starbucks seem to be
closing in as the place crowds,

but I'm hooked. Side effects?

*I feel nothing. Like that song!*
*After nine years of this,* she sings, *I feel nothing,*
*nothing, nothing at all…*

(A wreck is found
when a trawler pulses
in suspicious depths—the captain
pinging down a feeler
for sharpest dangers,
for shifting drecks.) So—

# 1-800-HOT-CHAT

It's such a dumb thing, a small thing. Right? I'm on the phone faking this guy out. Maybe some regular. He can't know that I pick toe jam out my toenails in this warehouse with maroon cubicles with soft grannies & few students in swivel chairs. He's just one more dumb small dud buying. Not touching. Just phone fucking me from a BBQ. Okay. It's June outside. *What's cooking?* I ask, hungry. *Halibut,* he laughs. *What's cooking with you?* I look around at the stale air. I've been losing weight the wrong way lately—without money. On my way in on my bike I saw a crowd at the bus stop & maybe no food made me think they swayed over some lady flat on her back on the sidewalk. Her fat feet in beige pumps stuck out over the curb. *That food sounds good. You should get some,* I say, picking fresh pimples & blotting pus with my sleeve. *Forget that,* he says & we chat about what we'd do but like kids do: *Let's pretend you do this. & then I do that.* Okay. Sometimes it doesn't work like when kids say, *You're dead!* & you say, *No I'm not!* But who decides? & this is what I want to know when I start hearing the BBQ. Kids closing in. Kids fading like running around. I hear a woman's question. *Flowers,* she says. There's his muffling hand, his slick whisper like a shrug or dad or door clicking. Then nothing. *Oooo-kaaaay,* he says, like he's my boyfriend's pal Trey who tells everyone I call him—chat hot when I don't. Would never. He's all *Oooo-kaaaay* the way he wasn't with Ms. Flowers. & I drop the receiver. Stop my desktop solitaire game. 'Cause I'm sick & froze & there's a kind of life behind his voice. & it's touching me.

## Some Things One "Escort" Talked About

1.Clients:

There's the "heavy" from his mother's basement. Clammy. Stupid. Sweet.
*I had to lift folds of flesh to find it.*
She'd bathe his grease off & be kind with kind words that always worked.

There's the "windsor knot." That silent addict—on time for his (breakfast, lunch,
   dinner) release.
For the ritual that screws him into his dry clean shirt, afterwards.
He has trimmed. He has yanked on his beveled black sock.

There's the "just hubby." Always for the awful hour. Married to his friend,
   "the mother." He likes their kids.
Likes to chat. Likes you smart. & this isn't cheating, *She's basically agreed.* He is legion.
He just won't go.

2.Boxes:

They'd say, *You came really hard!* She'd say, *No I didn't.* She could say that.
She could box them up
like dolls, like corpses she makes pretty for the family at the viewing.

# A 21st Century Slave to Her Master

*For I have but the power to kill,/ Without—the power to die...*
                                            —Emily Dickinson

*You need me. I know you.*
That's my kick. That I see
all of you above me
as a hairline pocked.
Wet with buttons
of grease.

Stop breathing
so hard. You get to buy.
You get to fade
into the townhouse
I imagine. I just kill
your need

& pretend it's a kick
I need. I remember,
as you rape me,
all that time I spent
mulling want
ads for exotics.

Like those were okay jobs;
like that'd be power.
For me.
I remember you
say, *Thanks...*
like I was real. Like you

don't stink.
Like the tatted devil
on the stair, john, you paid
to master me.
Like your death.
Your death—yeah

that's the shit.
Not some kick.
Not my rinky-dink
knowing you
over & over. The shit's
you handling me.

Like you would
a Colt, a Glock.
You aiming the sheen
thing at your temple.
Getting off
a clean shot.

So—
next time
at that whispered, *Where are you?*
I'll fill my husk
with coiled rope
& that plea will bounce
& return
to a Source. Then—*how sweet*

## Train

*We're not like them.* Phone-sex girls tease
men on the wire
for nickels on the minute,
for fractions of a penny on the word.
Their masterminded words
like vaginas, like wormholes, like succubi,
like the fingers of the animated
dead pushing men in little wagons
over a little hill. The men give a weak
*weeeeeeeeeee*, then crawl out the transport
still lonely. *We're not like them—*
*at least*, say phone-sex girls about
streetwalkers who stiletto
stomp down the block, follow through
on the threat—give a B.J. for a Grant,
a backdoor for a Benjamin—
who choose to quick kill
desire. Their men don't know the body
is the soul. *We are not*
*like them*, whisper streetwalkers about slaves
brought up from Tenancingo, from Odessa,
from Portland: girls tricked
& trafficked, locked up by fist,
by force fed dope, by "mamchkis"
or "boyfriends" or blockbusters
like Pretty Woman. *We're not like*
*them*, think some old slaves
about girls pimped by parents.
The daughters
who moan, *Mommy* while a train
of men shout, *Shut your fucking mouth.*

## Power Play

*Now, the serpent was more crafty than any other beast of the field…* -Genesis 3:1

The first sin was a pimp's
lie to a girl dazzled
by the glamour love
of a god—the glamour
of a grown-up rave,
of knowing, having, it all.

Then the pimp made Adam
into Eve's first drake. Knowing
these facts—you know history…

But, I should spell it:
the players—repeat

                repeat

                                repeat,

get shit, then
justify. *If you want to
sell yourself,* says the snake,
*That's empowerment.*

& the snake's got something—
she could be the Power.
The new-knowing one
leaning into Adam, hissing,
*Who's your daddy now.*

But, Adam can't think or feel
he's helpless, so he smacks her.

# The "John School"

This Baptist basement has low ceiling tiles.
Every john looks like his online mugshot.
Known. Some everyman
cognitive therapist gets up, says, *The world*

*is like a checkerboard*
*where buckets of crap occasionally*
*crash down from the sky.* He cackles. Motions.
About a hundred guys stir,

creak on a hundred fold-outs—
every numb butt shifting.
Some guys doodle. They cross
& uncross sneakers, loafers,

on pencil shavings. On loosed tobacco.
Then it's: here comes
the urologist in scrubs. He's got charts. *God…*
someone moans. Loudish.

A few men scratch something.
Scratch the next thing. The itch
just moves around to another patch of skin.
Then "Alexis" from a factory,

booked 80 plus times & shot
when hooking, gets up, says,
*You're no different than I was.*
Her small face is wrinkle free

under a purple wool hat,
*Everyone has to look*
*at the void they're trying to fill.*
Someone's wife gets up,

says *Gonorrhea* to the crowd. Her man
got 5 to 7 with that curse.
*& now, I can't...* she sighs, looks down
at a crumb & an ant on the concrete,

while the johns think, *Shit!*
or, *She knows...*or, *Just finish.*
A few guys don't blush.
A few do.

## Love All the Girls

*When asked what would end prostitution, one [POPPY Project] interviewee*
*laughed & said, "Kill all the girls."*

For instance, little "Minty" Ross.
If you kill her, she won't
see baby Moses
hidden from sale by her mother
Rit, won't know Rit's promise
that—*the first man*
*that comes into my house, I will*
*split his head open,* this girl will
not spark
& know to skedaddle,
or send along a song
to her mother in Maryland—
*I'll meet you*
*in the morning, I'm bound*

*for the promised land…*
If you kill her, she won't *North Star,*
nor conduct, nor stare at her hands
in free Philadelphia
to see if she was *the same*
*person,* she won't be crowned
General, nor own herself,
nor name herself
"Harriet Tubman,"
she will never unslave, untether,
hundreds & hundreds
at night, in war. This Ashanti,
this granddaughter of rape,
this scout, this spy, this girl
seized up & revealed—

if you kill her
the "Lion of God,"
of reason, Mr. Douglas,
will have no heart
to say—*the midnight sky*
*& the silent stars have been*
*the witnesses of your devotion*
*to freedom*, & Harriet
will never, about the Choptank River,
about that final footfall
after ninety miles,
reply—*the sun came like gold*
*through the trees, & over*
*the fields, & I felt like I was*
*in Heaven…*

*—how sweet*
the stop of stop-gaps
the waves cannot quite cross!)
*Sound saves!* Will save
the slimy thing that,
breached into air,
is golden, bold. The long-goneness

# Bird

*For survivors of abuse & trafficking residing at the Breaking Free safe house in Minneapolis, Minnesota.*

Rock Wren, Godwit, Bobolink?
What are we looking at?
What's beaked & broken
free from
a classic, iron
bell cage? With a blown-out hole
opposite a latched door? No

thickened keratin could peck that well. No
claw-turned-fist
busted up that joint.
Inside, she was key,
she was *cheep*, she was a flipped
bad finger. Now—this bird wings

as every bird
stepping out of "the life."
With no credit,
no reference, & a little self
love. What are we looking at?

A second wind. The flight
inside the creature
that is the holy, eternal
verb. Is:
who bent the metal. Is: the mother
of a lighter

bone. The kind
that terror
cannot allow.

# Thistle

*For survivors of abuse and trafficking residing at Thistle Farms
in Washington, D.C.*

Beloved of butterfly. Tint of
twilight. In the language of flora—

she is Regal. Sometimes called Spear
or Welted or Blessed—

sometimes Melancholy or
Milk. She is every third-grade girl

tying her shoes—all knee bone
& chin sharp. As tincture, she cures

buboes & baldness,
stone & gravel. As warrior bloom,

she defends the tribe
of tartaned folk with her fierce burrs.

Then we knead her into heel & shin.
She is Soft & Clean, a Delectable

Heart—centerpiece of sustenance
& no weed. O, taste of celery. Herb of witch.

In *War & Peace*, she is
the finale field. The constant, gorgeous

soul of us. The eyes of us, the Thriving.

## May 28th, 2014

*-For my husband*

Maya Angelou died today.
Farzana Iqbal was stoned by 20 men with bricks today.
Boko Haram hides & holds 219
school girls today. It has been 44 days. Maya
Angelou died today. 137 pages of
Elliot's Misogynist Manifesto have been
shredded—it's 6 days since Santa Barbara, since
he ravaged 19. Not all men,
some say. Yes all women, others say. Maya Angelou died
today. She was happy to go, I hear. She slept through it,
sweetly. The writer of the "Rape Joke" poem
made the *New York Times* today. & I cannot
love you. Would you say
what the song sings, when the song says,
*You are every women in the world*
*to me?* When I don't know you? When I can't
gift myself? I don't have words
for you. I know Maya Angelou died today. It's all over
the news. I know there are tender men.
Some are famous. (I'm thinking—Gandhi.)
The others die unknown. Like women,
they have moon faces. Phases. Everything
depends. They can be war. & I'm not antiwar,
per se. I just look like I am, like I look
like a vegetarian. I love men,
I think. Digesting is the trouble. I love you.
869 men earned their honor by killing
869 women in Pakistan. That's the number we know today.
But night is dark. We know Farzana died
with the daylight, on the steps of the highest court,
in the 2nd largest city, in front of 52 police,
lawyers, kin, men. What can I do? What
does loving you do? Should I write? I stood up today
at an open mic & someone said, Maya Angelou died
today. The poetry there was terrible.

But the 28 poets were happy. Ms. Angelou
was happy, too. What do I know? I get up
after 15 readers to read &
I've no power. I'm not happy. Farzana was
3 months pregnant. What good
are we? I'm not right. Maybe I'm not people. You are
every man. You are ugly. You've done nothing wrong.
We have a son. He's 11. Can I forgive him
for becoming a man? Not yet.
But you, Beautiful, did I tell you?
Precious & Hope ran from Boko Haram
in their Chibok school uniforms. Ran
through thorns. &, Maya weeps
at 86, telling Oprah,
"God loves me!" She says it over &
over & over. & I'm not thinking, *Oh god...*
It's more, *My God,*
*where are you?* &,
He's all, *Where the hell are you?*

## A Safe Home

//One day, C smiled, mixed cedar mulch & Atlanta loam with bare hands when the cool & the green smelled like home. //One day, D dropped a Snapple bottle cap on kitchen tile & her toddler son took it, spun it, again & again, till her laughter echoed off the stucco walls of their home. //One day, F settled twins down to nap then stretched across an armchair in the sun because the heat & the bright felt like a blanket at home. //One day, the hottest day, G's daughter was cut from her uterus & placed in her arms, where the infant's spiked hair slanted right with the texture of home. //One day, J exhaled, climbed a step to a stage, read her poem, & forgot the eyes of the crowd when the words tasted fine, when the words were a home. //One day, K stood on a stool with a spoon, helped her grandma stir pea soup, helped her shred cheese, & the steaming orange on her tongue melted smooth like home. //One day, L let a drumbeat shake her hips—left-left, right-right—& she spun in heels, arms hugging sisters, as she danced at home. //One day, M rolled out of bed into a pre-dawn living room to see boxes & boxes, & all the sparkle & red & pine & yes of her home. //One day, O saw a chocolate chip cookie planet in the Space Mountain sky as she screamed a smile on that rollercoaster as the roll-bar kept her homed. //One day, P sang the grace song, & the lamb or the holy shivered up her skin, tickled her chords, & came out loud & strong, at home. //One day, a rainy day, S put her pen & pad to work at a bus stop & one side of a big grin bloomed when "some" followed "home." //One day, T was clowning in class, so the girls in the back cracked up & she busted a gut at how her words hit home. //One day, V let her shoulders down, let herself be the right one for the job, let the desk & the calls & the emails be as natural as home. //One day, W took a hardback off a library shelf, cracked the spine, split the pages, & wondered at words giving shape to a girl with a flash-light, to a mystery like home. //One day, Z saw her son move a tassel from one side to another, grip a rolled-up sheaf, smile at the camera, at her—because she meant home. //

goneness

& the longing cleans
that me—
no matter tear & wear.

# Notes

**"Dear Jasz,"** is an epistolary based on an interview that I conducted for the Amirah blog with survivor-advocate & modern-day abolitionist Jasmine Grace Marino, author of *The Diary of Jasmine Grace*.

**"Garden of Truth"** was written in response to a study titled "Garden of Truth: The Prostitution & Trafficking of Native Women in Minnesota," which was compiled by Melissa Farley, Nicole Matthews, Sarah Deer, Guadalupe Lopez, Christine Stark, & Eileen Hudon. It is a project of Minnesota Indian Women's Sexual Assault Coalition & Prostitution Research & Education & was released by William Mitchell College of Law in Saint Paul, Minnesota in October 2011. This study is incredibly important given that a disproportionate percentage of the women arrested for prostitution in America identify as American Indian while American Indians comprise a miniscule percentage of the total population.

**"May 28th, 2014"** is dedicated to all my SDOP (Student Day of Poetry) students who participated in my "Great News!" workshops at Mass Poetry. It is also dedicated to the gracious, elegant, inspiring woman & poet: Maya Angelou.

**"Object Lesson"** is dedicated to Afaa Michael Weaver & was inspired by his poem "The Appaloosa."

**"The 'John School'"** is dedicated to Norma Hotaling—a survivor-advocate, former homeless prostitute, & co-founder of SAGE (Standing Against Global Exploitation) & co-founder of The First Offender Prostitution Program, which was the first "john school" in America. The poem is based on articles about a "john school" in Nashville TN; & quotes the school's director Kenny Baker.

**"When I taught poetry at the safe house"** & **"A Safe Home"** are dedicated to residents & advocates of Amirah, which, according to their website, "strives to provide a refuge for those seeking to break free from exploitation & heal in community on their journey toward lasting hope. [They] do this by providing safe homes for those that want to break free from sexual exploitation, mobilizing the greater community to create opportunities for healing, restoration & reintegration."

# Acknowledgments

Infinite gratitude to Julie Shematz – founder of the survivor advocacy organization Beauty From Ashes™ – who provided the cover art, which is titled: "Self-Discipline II".

Many thanks to the following journals where these poems first appeared in earlier versions or with different titles:

*Crab Creek Review*: "Amazing Grace" (which is scattered throughout the book)
*Green Mountains Review*: "Exchange"
*Drunk Monkeys*: "Some Things One Escort Talked About"
*Ibbetson Street Magazine*: "Love All the Girls"
*The Lily Poetry Review*: "Dear Jasz"
*Oddball Magazine*: "May 28th, 2014"
*Pangyrus*: "1-800-HOT-CHAT"
*The Philadelphia Review of Books*: "A 21st Century Slave to Her Master"
*Pirene's Fountain*: "The 'John' School"
*Rattle Magazine*: "Bird" & "#CarryThatWeight"
*Rise Up Review*: "Object Lesson"
*SWWIM*: *"Escort' is her word &"*
*Waxwing*: "Power Play" & "Object"

Special thanks to Angelika Selle, president of Women's Federation for World Peace USA, who read "Power Play" at the 2013 Universal Peace Federation Forum: "Human Trafficking & Poverty, a Critical Connection."

As well, thanks to the editors at *Broadsided Press* for printing "Thistle" in broadside format; to the editors of *Veils, Halos, & Shackles: an Anthology on the Abuse & Oppression of Women* (Kasva Press), for publishing "Train"; to the editors of *The Anatomy of Silence* (Red Press), for publishing "Exchange"; &, to the editors of *Shout it Out! an anthology of poems against domestic violence* (Lost Tower), for reprinting "Bird."

& heapfulls of appreciation to the Salem Writers Group and others who were the first to take brave steps to read through and help me perfect (as much as was possible) these poems and the larger series of poems from which these were drawn: January O'Neil, Jennifer Martelli, Cindy Veach, Laurette Folk, Dawn Paul, Kevin Carey, J.D. Scrimgeour, Maggie Smith,

Kelli Agodon, and Enzo Surin. Also—Sebastien, Luc, Chloe, Mom—I could not have written anything at all without your support!

Finally, sincere thanks to IJN who sparked this project; and to interviewees A & C & D & F & G—for offering up their time, their stories, & their truth. May God bless & keep safe every thriver at every safe home. & may we all nurture hope.

ABOUT THE AUTHOR

Jennifer Jean's honors include: a Peter Taylor Fellowship from the Kenyon Review Writers Workshop; a Disquiet Fellowship from Dzanc Books; and an Ambassador for Peace Award from the Women's Federation for World Peace. Her poems and co-translations appear in: *POETRY, Waxwing, Rattle, Crab Creek, DMQ, On the Seawall, Salamander,* and *The Common.* She is the author of the full length collection *THE FOOL.* Jennifer edits translations for *Talking Writing* and Her Story Is; and, is a consulting editor for the *Kenyon Review* and the founder of Free2Write Poetry Workshops for Trauma Survivors.

CPSIA information can be obtained
at www.ICGtesting.com
Printed in the USA
JSHW031739301220
10618JS00003B/158